Your Amazing Body

Teeth

by Imogen Kingsley

Bullfrog Books

Ideas for Parents and Teachers

Bullfrog Books let children practice reading informational text at the earliest reading levels. Repetition, familiar words, and photo labels support early readers.

Before Reading

- Discuss the cover photo. What does it tell them?

- Look at the picture glossary together. Read and discuss the words.

Read the Book

- "Walk" through the book and look at the photos. Let the child ask questions. Point out the photo labels.

- Read the book to the child, or have him or her read independently.

After Reading

- Prompt the child to think more. Ask: Do you enjoy biting into a crunchy apple? What other foods are fun to bite?

Bullfrog Books are published by Jump!
5357 Penn Avenue South
Minneapolis, MN 55419
www.jumplibrary.com

Library of Congress Cataloging-in-Publication Data

Names: Kingsley, Imogen, author.
Title: Teeth / by Imogen Kingsley.
Description: Minneapolis, MN: Jump!, Inc., 2017.
Series: Your amazing body
Audience: Ages 5–8. | Audience: K to grade 3.
Includes bibliographical references and index.
Identifiers: LCCN 2016051870 (print)
LCCN 2016052895 (ebook)
ISBN 9781620316900 (hardcover: alk. paper)
ISBN 9781620317433 (pbk.)
ISBN 9781624965678 (ebook)
Subjects: LCSH: Teeth—Juvenile literature.
Anatomy—Juvenile literature.
Classification: LCC QM311 .K57 2017 (print)
LCC QM311 (ebook) | DDC 612.3/11—dc23
LC record available at https://lccn.loc.gov/2016051870

Editor: Jenny Fretland VanVoorst
Book Designer: Molly Ballanger
Photo Researcher: Molly Ballanger

Photo Credits: Alamy: Eric Raptosh Photography, 10. Getty: JGI, cover. Shutterstock: Brocreative, 1; David Svetlik, 3; Photographee.eu, 4, 5; s_oleg, 4, 5; CREATISTA, 6–7; aekkorn, 8–9; All About Space, 8–9; Deyan Georgiev, 12–13; bikeriderlondon, 14–15; Trudy Wilkerson, 14–15; Casezy idea, 16–17; Littlekidmoment, 18; Claudio Divizia, 19; Lilya Espinosa, 19; Monkey Business Images, 20–21; Tefi, 22; Africa Studio, 24. SuperStock: Blend Images, 7. Thinkstock: Big Cheese Photo, 11.

Printed in the United States of America at Corporate Graphics in North Mankato, Minnesota.

Table of Contents

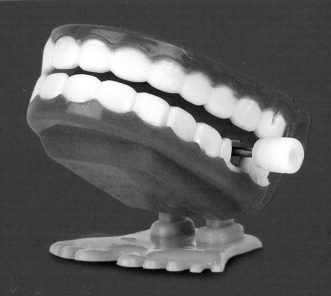

Crunch! Chomp!

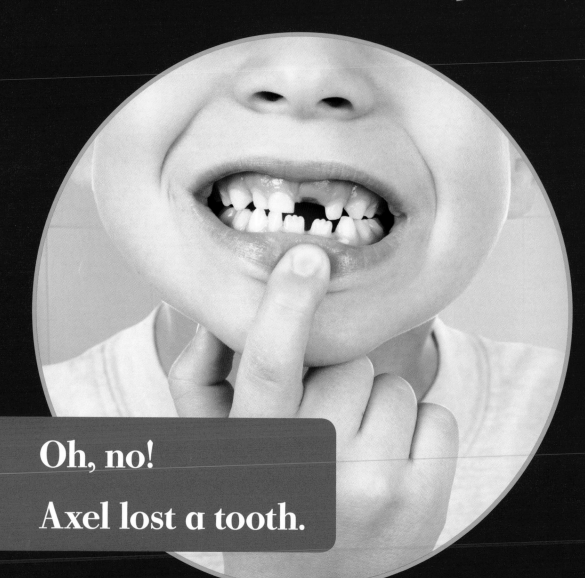

Oh, no!

Axel lost a tooth.

It is OK.

It is a baby tooth.

A big one will grow in.

baby tooth

5

Why do we need teeth?
Teeth help us talk.

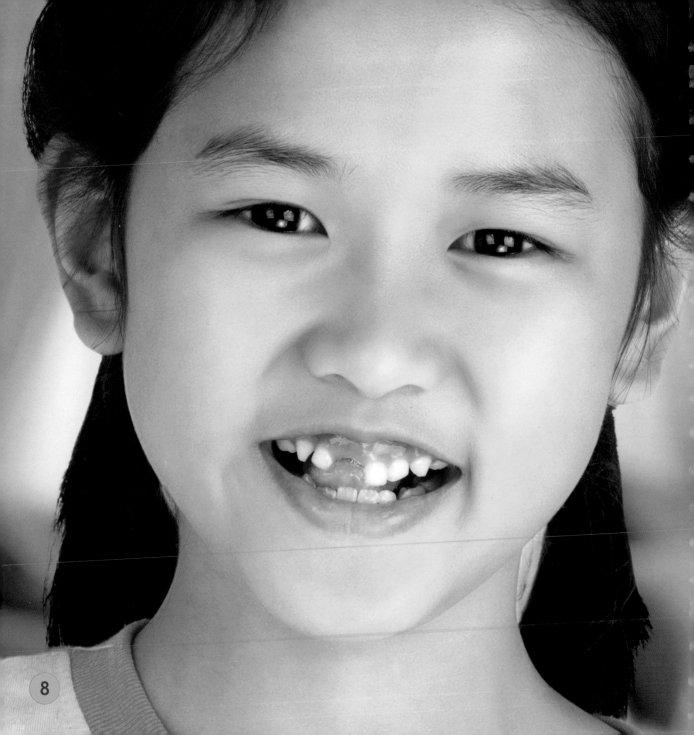

Say "This tooth is loose."

Your tongue
hits your teeth.

They help
make sounds.

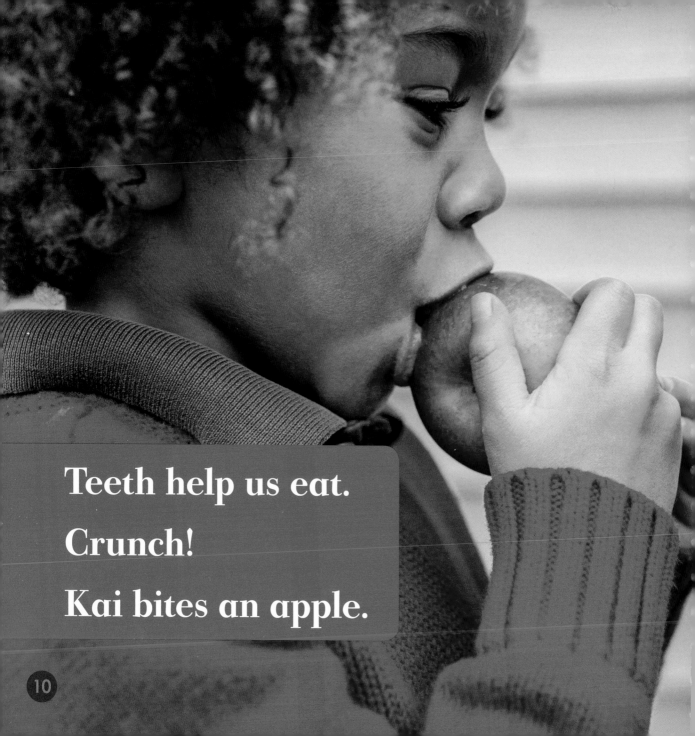

Teeth help us eat.
Crunch!
Kai bites an apple.

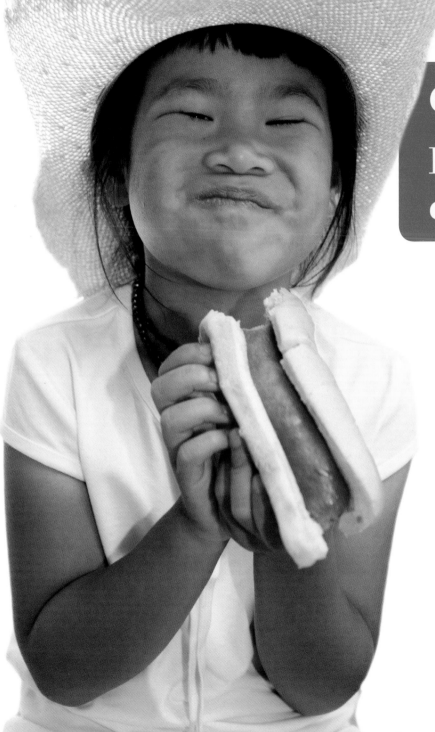

Chomp!
Bo grinds
a hot dog.

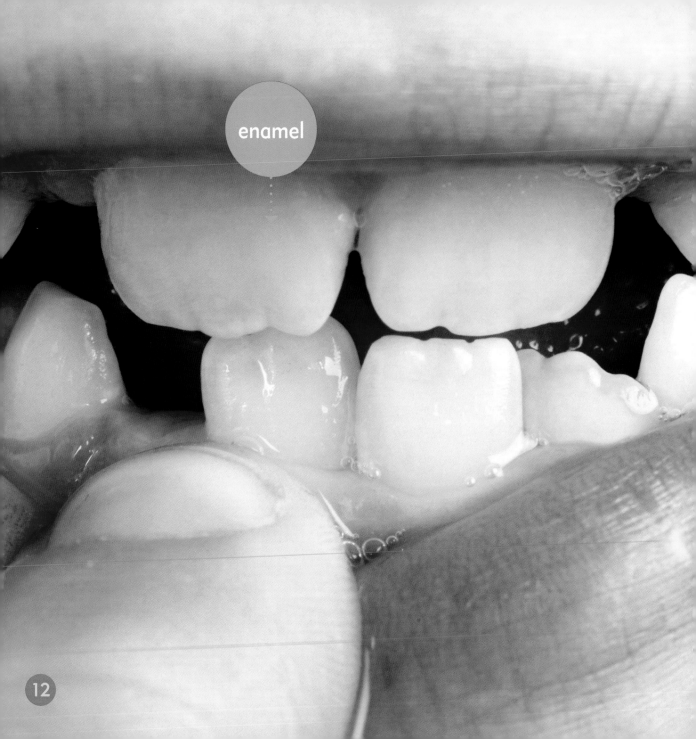

enamel

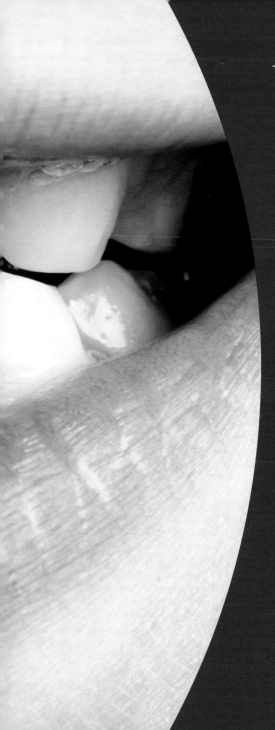

Your teeth are strong.

They are covered
in enamel.

It is the hardest
thing in your body.

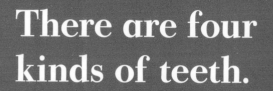

There are four
kinds of teeth.

Each kind has a job.

Incisors are in front.

They cut food.

incisor

canine

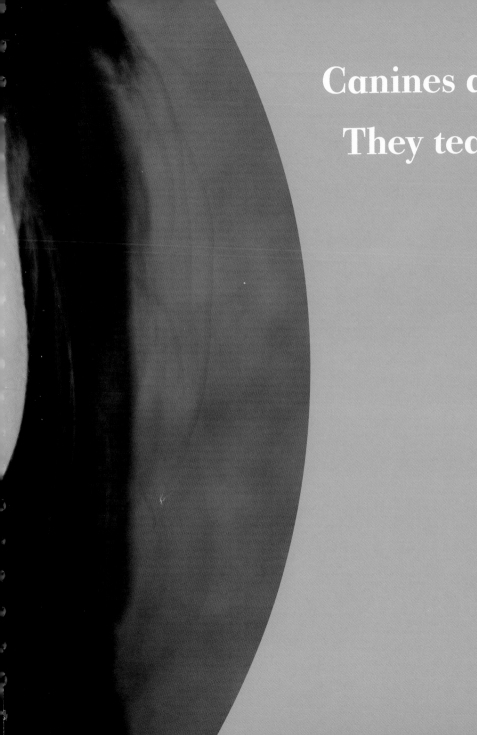

Canines are sharp.

They tear food.

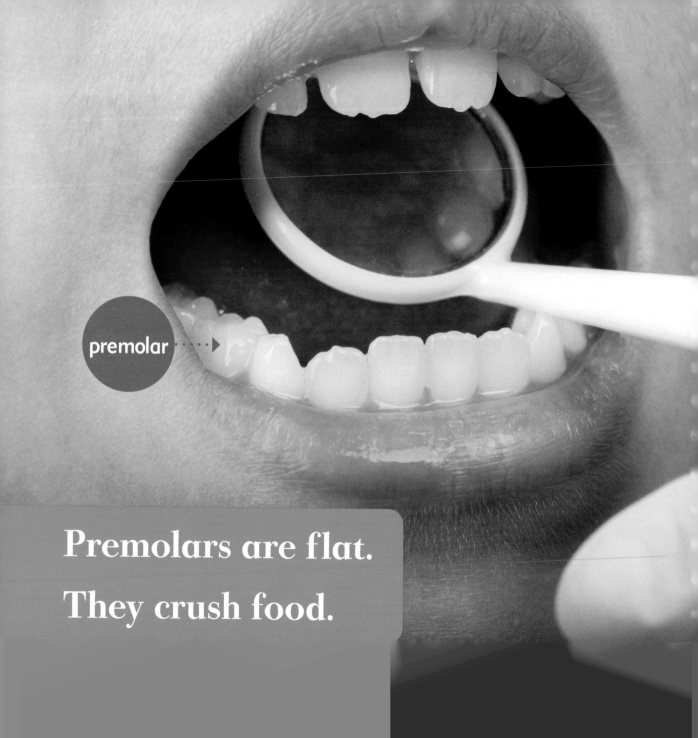

premolar ····▶

Premolars are flat.

They crush food.

Molars are
in the back.

They are big.

They grind food.

molar

19

What else do teeth
help us do?

Smile!

Parts of a Tooth

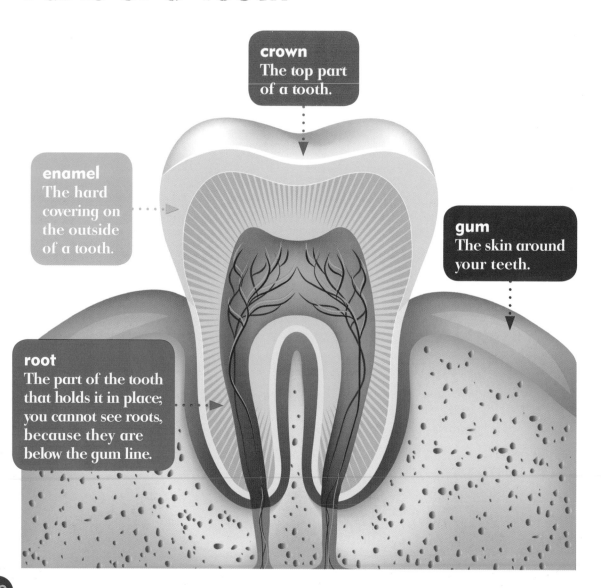

crown
The top part of a tooth.

enamel
The hard covering on the outside of a tooth.

gum
The skin around your teeth.

root
The part of the tooth that holds it in place; you cannot see roots, because they are below the gum line.

Picture Glossary

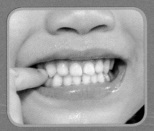

canines
Long, sharp teeth used for ripping food. There are two on top and two on the bottom.

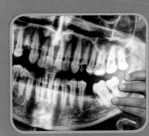

molars
Your biggest teeth, found in the back of your mouth. They are used for grinding and chewing food.

incisors
Your front teeth are the first to come in. There are four on top and four on the bottom.

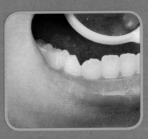

premolars
Premolars are sometimes called bicuspids. They are used for crushing food.

Index

To Learn More

Learning more is as easy as 1, 2, 3.

1) Go to www.factsurfer.com

2) Enter "teeth" into the search box.

3) Click the "Surf" button to see a list of websites.

With factsurfer.com, finding more information is just a click away.